PUT ME IN COACH
Living a Bold Life

JOHN W. STANKO

urbanpress

Put Me In Coach
by John W. Stanko
Copyright © 2019 John W. Stanko

ISBN # 978-1-63360-130-7

All rights reserved under International Copyright Law. Written permission must be secured from the publisher/author to reproduce, copy, or transmit any part of this book.

For Worldwide Distribution Printed in the U.S.A.

Urban Press
P.O. Box 8881
Pittsburgh, PA 15221-0881 USA
412.646.2780
www.urbanpress.us

INTRODUCTION

I wrote this book because I continue to be concerned about the passivity I encounter from believers who are content to attend church and watch others play the purpose game. That's why the "Put Me In, Coach" emphasis emerged, for I want to encourage you to stop being content to watch the game. Instead, actively seek to play the game, whatever the game is for you, be it teaching, traveling, writing, dancing, giving, or fixing. If you are waiting for an engraved invitation to do any of those things, you will wait a long time for something that will never come. God has already issued all the invitations there will be, and you don't *have* to RSVP you are going to be involved, you *get* to RSVP. It's a privilege to serve the Lord.

We have been steeped in a theology that says there is no good thing that dwells in any of us. I certainly agree this is true—concerning the time *before* we know and serve the Lord. After we surrender our lives to Him, He is present to produce in us the good fruit that comes from obedience and surrender. We all have gifts and those gifts are not for ourselves—they are for the benefit of others. I want my gifts to impact others for good, and that means I have to acknowledge, develop, and then express them as often as possible.

That means my gifts may be operating and I am not even aware they are and the same is true for you. I am a teacher and I find myself teaching even when I am not aware I am doing so. When I model certain behaviors, people see them and are being instructed in the way to live and work.

I determined years ago that God had permission to use *anything* within my being—my gifts, work, presence, words, writing—to help other people. He did not need my permission and I did not need to be aware of the beneficial results. I was no longer going to deny what I could do well and pretend like I enjoyed or was effective at what I did not do well. I was done pretending like I was not effective in a certain area when I knew I was, all in the attempt to be perceived as humble. When I deny what I can do in the interests of appearing humble, then that is not humility. It is false humility and that does not honor God, for I was denying what He had done in my life and who He has made me to be.

God can make any of us public figures and He does not need our permission. He can make our gifts and impact as significant as He chooses, and it's none of our business. Our response is to cooperate and make sure our character and the excellence of our gifts are what they need to be.

What are you about to read is a collection of *Monday Memos* I published in late 2018 and early 2019 to build a case that God is waiting for us to involve ourselves in His work. He does direct us, sometimes clearly and specifically, but at other times we are free to volunteer and God won't be offended when we do. I am not sure how and when I started saying, "Put Me In, Coach," but when I shared it with some of my college classes, the students picked up on it and began to say it to me and others whenever someone was hesitant to do God's will as they understood it.

Put Me In, Coach is not a mantra; it's a prayer and I invite you to pray it with me and then get ready through practice and gameday simulations to play the real game, which involves serving others and touching lives as His representatives. I no longer am content to sit on the sidelines or the grandstand. I want to be in the game, and I hope I run into you on the field.

John W. Stanko
Pittsburgh, PA
November 2019

PUT ME IN, COACH

In December of 2018, I conducted what I labeled a "purpose revival" on Facebook, posting more than 100 short inspirational and challenging posts over a three-day period. The concept caught fire and captured attention from around the world. One of the themes during the revival that struck a chord with readers was my thread called "put me in, coach!" It is that topic that I want to examine in this book and first chapter.

Here Am I, Send Me.

Let's start by looking at Isaiah 6:4-9a:

> And the posts of the door were shaken by the voice of him who cried out, and the house was filled with smoke. So I said: "Woe is me, for I am undone! Because I am a man of unclean lips, And I dwell in the midst of a people of unclean lips; For my eyes have seen the King, the Lord of hosts." Then one of the seraphim flew to me, having in his hand a live coal which he had taken with the tongs from the altar. And he touched my mouth with it, and said: "Behold, this has touched your lips; Your iniquity is

taken away, and your sin purged." Also I heard the voice of the Lord, saying: "Whom shall I send, And who will go for Us?" Then I said, "Here am I! Send me." He said, "Go and tell this people . . ."

This passage has important lessons if you are looking for God to use you while have the put-me-in-coach attitude. Let's quickly examine those lessons:

1. When confronted with God's presence, Isaiah felt woefully inadequate, uttering the phrase "woe is me."

2. God touched Isaiah and cleansed, empowered, and energized what Isaiah felt to be his biggest weakness: his lips.

3. God took away Isaiah's iniquity and sin with one touch of a coal from His altar.

4. After the cleansing process, which was not a long, drawn-out event, the Lord asked who would be willing to go to speak to the people on His behalf.

5. Isaiah immediately volunteered and God sent him without hesitation or reservation.

What can we learn from this story that will enable God to use us as He did Isaiah?

Ready to Play the Game

A number of years ago, I was confronted by my own fear of God using me because I didn't feel I was ready. I was waiting for someone to "discover" me so I would not seem to be self-promoting if I stepped forward to say, "I'm ready. I can do that." I was waiting on the Lord but going nowhere, and felt like something was missing. Indeed, there was.

What was missing was the courage to accept who God had made me to be and what He wanted me to do. When I realized my fear, I immediately stopped putting my faith in my preparations and also stopped surrendering the sovereignty of my life to others who had no idea what was in my heart or what God had called me to do. I had experience, education, and a heart to serve the Lord any-place in the world He wanted me to go. At that point, I said, "Put me in, Coach. I'm ready." That didn't mean I was finished with personal development, but it did mean I was ready to play God's game and learn not from the sideline but by being engaged and involved.

Isaiah's problem—his lips—was dealt with in an in-stant. God empowered and equipped him for the mission, but God did not send him off. Isaiah had to make himself available by volunteering to go. In essence, Isaiah said, "Put me in, Lord!" God heard him and granted his request and we are still being impacted by what took place.

Is it time that you stopped being content with being a bench player or worse yet, a spectator? What is keeping you from getting into the game of your life purpose? In all probability, it is fear that you aren't ready or that you are getting ahead of the Lord's will for your life. My advice to you is that you may not be as ready as you are going to be, but you're ready now to do more than you're doing. I urge you to change your thinking from "I'm not ready; I need more time" to "put me in, coach" and see what the Lord does and how He uses you.

TOUCHED BY YOUR WORK

In this chapter, let's look at a passage that goes along with the put-me-in-coach theme and it's found in Acts 19:11-12: "God did extraordinary miracles through Paul, so that even handkerchiefs and aprons that had touched him were taken to the sick, and their illnesses were cured and the evil spirits left them." If you are like me, you may look at this story and think it is a bizarre manifestation of how the Spirit once worked, but I think it's much more than that, and is a pattern for how God wants to use us right now.

Work Things

This passage can make us uncomfortable because of how some have applied the concept. We have heard of people who promised to send out a prayer cloth over which the prophet or healer has prayed, which was guaranteed to produce results in the recipient's life—if only that person would send a donation to the sending ministry. I once saw a ministry send out a shower cap with a red outline of a hand on top with the promise that when the recipient wore the cap in the shower, the sender's hand would be on them to bless them while they bathed. We know that's silliness and we have run in the opposite direction (rightly so) to never be involved in that foolishness.

The zaniness of how others have applied these verses, however, does not diminish the fact that God used Paul's aprons and hankies to heal and deliver others. I don't know if people had Paul's permission to use his things in this way. Maybe they went into his work area or personal effects, took his work clothes and other items, and went off to pray for people, without Paul even knowing. Perhaps he endorsed and initiated their actions, but whatever Paul's disposition toward this, people were helped and God was glorified.

What are the lessons for us from this story?

The Lessons

The main lesson is this: You have *no right* to hold on to something if God can use it to help others. If your words, poems, presence, ideas, perspective, prayers, gifts, purpose, or insight can benefit someone, you have an obligation to get them out there so others can benefit from their use. What's more, once you put them out there, people are free to use them as they see fit and you lose control of whatever it was you shared and made available—just like Paul's personal items.

When I write a book, one person can buy it and share it with 20 people. I get no financial return from that, but my work can then touch, heal, and deliver 20 people. I *want* that to happen. Someone could even take my ideas and write their own book with using my ideas and teaching, thus helping more people. What am I do to then? Bring a lawsuit against the author? No, that author took my hankie and apron (so to speak), touched others, and made them well. I am not to *resist* that; I am to *cooperate* if that happens. Who knows, maybe that author will do a better job than I did, but at least they will touch people in their world who are not part of mine.

When I publish something on social media, people are free to share it however they wish. They can even mess it up or distort it, but that's the risk I take when I commit something to God by putting it out there beyond my reach or control. In a sense, I am not saying "Put me in, Coach" but I am saying, "Put my stuff in, Coach. Use it as You see fit, which includes not using it at all."

Years ago, I complained to the Lord that my books were not selling well. He spoke to me and said, "Who said you have to sell them?" That changed my thinking and showed me that I was to stop controlling my stuff but was to put it out there by whatever means possible. That attitude has complemented my philosophy of "Put me in, Coach" quite nicely, and that is why you see me all over social media, always looking for a way to touch more people with my life lessons, humor, and fruit. If someone has a problem with that, well, that's their problem, and I urge them to read Acts 19:11-2 to see that I am only following what the early church did with Paul's things—with or without his permission.

CHAPTER 3

YOUR SPIRITUAL SHADOW

This book, *Put Me In, Coach*, is my story of how I overcame my fears to allow God to use me more often than He was—or more often than I was allowing Him to. I had to get over my fears that I didn't know enough, wasn't prepared enough, or wasn't spiritual enough. I realized that those assessments were mine and not necessarily God's, and I concluded if I wasn't ready, I would *never* be ready. I also concluded that part of my growth was not only to study the game and learn, but to *play* the game and learn—and the game was ministry, writing, and teaching, not just locally but all over the world. The game for me was my purpose and I presented myself to the Lord for Him to use as He saw fit, not according to how I saw myself.

The rest is history, as they say, and the results have been the most fulfilling and productive years of my life. In all probability, you are ready and capable of doing more than you allow yourself to believe, and this book is devoted to help you get rid of the mentality I had that prevented me from playing in God's purpose game. In the last chapter, we looked at a story in Paul's life and in this one we will look at a story from Peter's life, both of which are designed to help you say, "Put me in, Coach!" Here goes.

Your Shadow

In psychology, there is a concept called the shadow side. It is a side of our personality of which we are unaware or choose to ignore, but that doesn't mean it isn't active. People may encounter our shadow side every time they come in contact with us—something like our sarcasm, competitiveness, need to control, fear, or greed. You can see why we tend to ignore those things, for they are usually not all that positive. Until we can bring those shadows into the light, they continue to operate and can damage our relationships, work, and ministry, and do so from a subconscious level.

While you probably have a negative shadow, did you know you also have a positive or spiritual one? It's the good residue you leave whenever people have an encounter with you—and it also can be something of which you are not aware. While the psychological shadow is usually harmful or negative, your spiritual shadow can be positive and leave a lasting impression for good. Acts 5:15 describes people who had an encounter with the Apostle Peter's positive shadow (even though his negative shadow had caused him to overestimate his loyalty to the Lord and led to his denial of Jesus): "People brought the sick into the streets and laid them on beds and mats so that at least Peter's shadow might fall on some of them as he passed by."

People get too hung up on the spooky spiritual side of this story, but I take it to heart by praying, "Lord, help me recognize my negative shadow, so my positive one—all the encounters with others I underestimate or of which I am not even conscious—can impact others with your love and for Your glory."

Be A God Carrier

In chapter two, we looked at a story found later in Acts: "God did extraordinary miracles through Paul, so that even handkerchiefs and aprons that had touched him were taken to the sick, and their illnesses were cured and the evil spirits left them" (Acts 19:11-12). Someone went into Paul's workshop, took his work apron, allowed people to touch it, and those people were healed. That leads me to another prayer: "Lord, I want my work to touch people whether I am present or not. Use my life—my writing, speaking, teaching, and every other activity—in a way that brings healing to peoples' lives, whether physical, emotional, or spiritual."

My goal is to be a God-carrier wherever I go and in whatever I do. I want my shadow and my work—the extension of my purpose and presence—to go with me, before me, and remain after me so God can use them for His purposes. If that means I must make myself personally available for people to touch my shadow or my apron, so be it. My life is His and I will not worship at the altar of privacy if God wants me to go public. In other words, my prayer or mantra is, "Put me in, Coach!"

I urge you to join me in praying those two prayers, and then develop your shadow, life's work, and gifts to such an extent that God can use them all to bring healing and help to hurting people.

CHAPTER 4

PURPOSE
GLORY

In this book, we are following a theme I have titled "Put Me in, Coach." We have focused on our need to prepare ourselves and then make ourselves available for God's purpose, even volunteering for service. In John 12:42-43, we read,

> "Nevertheless, many even of the authorities believed in him, but for fear of the Pharisees they did not confess it, so that they would not be put out of the synagogue; for they loved the glory that comes from man more than the glory that comes from God" (ESV).

Notice that the writer did not say Jesus' followers should not seek glory; he said they should not seek it from the wrong sources. Let's examine this concept a bit further in this chapter.

Airport Encounters

When I was in Santiago, Cuba years ago, a man came up to me and studied my face for a few seconds before he asked, "Are you John Stanko?" When I assured him I was, he informed me that he had heard me speak in Los Angeles a few years back and still remembered what I had spoken about, which of course was purpose. He then thanked God for the message and informed me that he had indeed found and was fulfilling his purpose. I also thanked God and left that encounter even more committed to spread the purpose gospel.

Yet, I also left that chance meeting with a renewed love for being recognized when I am in public. Once I was in an African airport and a man walked up to me, opened his briefcase, pulled out one of my books he was reading, and asked if I would autograph it and pose for a picture. I agreed to both and was exhilarated by his requests. I then thanked God that He had enabled me to touch that man's life through the purpose message in one of my books.

Then I was on a moving sidewalk in the Baltimore airport when a man moving in the other direction, yelled out, "Are you John Stanko? I read your book!" I smiled and waved back, wondering which book he was referring to, but thanking God once again that I had made a difference in someone's life. Those encounters are what have kept me writing, and at last count, I have published 42 books, including a few I have re-written.

In all three cases, I received a measure of glory in the form of recognition and praise. I was identified for who I was and what I had done for God that impacted others, and I was not uncomfortable with the experience. In fact, I wanted more—more recognition and more impact on people's lives. In a sense, you could say that I wanted (and still want) more glory. That's why I say regularly, "Put me in, Coach!"

Purpose Glory

I have written about the topic of self-promotion, and we will cover that later in this book. I took on that study because I was often accused of promoting myself when I talked about my books or travels. I wanted to look at what the Bible said about the subject, for most were convinced they already knew—thus, the label they applied to me.

Jesus said it was a problem to seek glory from the

wrong source (people) but permissible to seek it from the correct source (God). The safest way to obtain this glory is the same way that Jesus did, as described in John 17:4: "I glorified you on earth, *having accomplished the work that you gave me to do*" (ESV, emphasis added).

The glory I described in my three examples I refer to as purpose glory. It is the recognition and impact that we receive when we function in our purpose. Today, I have a publishing company and I know I have helped people publish who otherwise would not have been able to do so. When they announce their books on social media, they thank God for their finished book project. God is glorified through the work I do (and their work as well), and then they also thank me for my role. God and I formed a partnership with the author that brought God glory as I fulfilled my purpose, and I shared that glory with others. When I did, God was not offended, angered, or slighted in the least.

You will not give God glory by singing about it, saying the word "glory" in a worship setting, or reading about it in your Bible. You will not give God glory if you are afraid that some of it may spill over on to you, thus staining your righteous garments and offending and angering God. God cannot get glory unless you do something that causes others to acknowledge His work in and through you that benefited and blessed their lives. Therefore, you need to "get over yourself" and your hangup about drawing attention to yourself, and start drawing attention to yourself in a good way—by seeking the glory that comes from God, a glory that is connected to engaging and finishing the work He gave you to do. When you are ready to participate in this glory exchange, ask the Lord to "put me in, Coach," and then get ready for results that will indeed give God glory.

CHAPTER 5

CALL YOUR OWN NUMBER

This book is designed to help you overcome hesitation or fear of volunteering or enthusiastically embracing your purpose and creativity. Obviously, I am borrowing quite a few lessons and analogies from the sports world, but make no mistake, those lessons are applicable to real-life situations where we have a chance to serve the Lord by doing what it is we love to do and often do well.

It's not Pride

I was at a wedding recently where I met the father of the bride who is a medical doctor. He is in the Navy Reserves and every chance he gets, he volunteers to go to danger zones in Afghanistan or some other war-torn area to serve as a surgeon. I did not get a chance to talk to him much, but I heard from others that the only reason he was home at this time was because his daughter was getting married.

This man was calling his own number, which is a sports term to describe when someone puts themselves in a game with or without being asked to go in. (The coach says, "Number 24, you're in," and they wear number 24). It can also refer to when a player designates that he or she, and no one else, will take the important shot or kick at a crucial time in the game. The doctor I met was calling his own number when he decided he was going to serve rather than waiting to be called upon to serve.

It isn't pride for him to do so, nor is it pride when you do the same thing in your area of expertise, gifting, or purpose. In fact, there are many biblical examples of those who volunteered when they saw situations they knew they could address or help, and they did so without necessarily waiting for an invitation. In essence, they were calling their own number.

Examples

Here are some biblical examples I can identify of calling-your-own-number actions:

1. In 1 Samuel 17, David volunteered to take on Goliath. If you read the account, at no point are we told that the Lord spoke to David and directed him to fight. David came, assessed the situation, reviewed his past success killing lions and bears, and said, "I will fight Goliath." David called his own number.

2. We saw in the first chapter that Isaiah responded in Isaiah 6:1-8 to the Lord's question, "Who will go for us" by saying, "Here am I, send me!" Isaiah called his own number.

3. Paul wrote in 1 Timothy 3:1, "Here is a trustworthy saying: Whoever aspires to be an overseer desires a noble task." Paul did not write, "If you want to be an overseer, you need to curb your ambitions and wait on the Lord." He said it was a good thing to desire leadership, and went on to describe the characteristics a person would need to cultivate to become an overseer. The desire to lead was their way of calling their own number.

4. While the army of Israel was paralyzed

with fear, in 1 Samuel 14 we are told how Jonathan decided to climb the cliffs and lead the army to victory. He was so uncertain of whether his idea would succeed that he said "perhaps" the Lord would deliver them, and then asked for a sign to confirm his idea. Once he got his confirmation, Jonathan called his own number.

5. Paul did not advise the Corinthians to only look to Jesus as a model for their behavior. He wrote, "Follow my example, as I follow the example of Christ" (1 Corinthians 11:1). Paul drew attention to himself as a good role model to follow for those who were under his authority. He called his own number as a role model and teacher.

6. When Lydia came to the Lord in Acts 16:11-40, she insisted that Paul and his traveling party stay at her home. Later, she was a source of encouragement and provision for Paul as he traveled to other venues. Lydia called her own number and became a significant influence in the Philippian church.

7. When Nabal lived up to his name that meant "fool," his wife Abigail quickly prepared a picnic for David and his men and interceded on her husband's behalf. The Lord didn't tell her to do that. She acted quickly and prevented David from seeking revenge (see 1 Samuel 25). She also called her own number.

My point in offering these examples is to prove that God is not offended when we step up and call our own number. When we see an orphan and say, "I will feed them," God is pleased. When we see a need and have the resources and skill to make a difference and fill it, God is not threatened. I have established six libraries in Kenya, collecting books and shipping them over at great expense. The Lord did not tell me to do this, but my partners in Kenya asked if I could help. I figured God must have sent them so I called my own number and said, "I'll help."

In what area of your life are you ready to step up and play the game? Where is there an opening on a team where you can come forward to say, "I can help. I'll serve"? Wherever or whatever it is, I urge you to call your own number and put yourself in the game, then go about winning in that area for the glory of God.

CHAPTER 6

SELF-PROMOTION 1

Let's continue our discussion around the theme, "Put Me In, Coach," which is examining the concept of putting yourself forward as ready, willing, and able to fulfill your purpose and express your gifts. I regularly have discussions with people concerned about writing a book or stepping out into other purpose work because they feel they may be promoting themselves rather than the Lord. They are worried (yes, worried is the correct word) they will get ahead of the Lord, or somehow do something that brings glory to self instead of glory to God. Those are legitimate concerns, but are all based and rooted in fear, and we know that God has not given us a spirit of fear.

About ten years ago, I did a series titled "Self-Promotion," so I thought it would be good to revisit that topic in light of the concerns that my friends have recently raised, which are consistent with the "Put Me In, Coach" discussion. It's an issue I have pondered for a long time, since I have been labeled as self-promoting from time to time, so I am eager to share my thoughts with you.

Conceit

The main concern with self-promotion is best summarized in Philippians 2:3, where Paul wrote: "Do nothing out of selfish ambition or vain conceit. Rather, in humility value others above yourselves." Many conclude talking about oneself in almost any situation is wrong or at least improper, and ambition is also considered to be in bad taste or downright evil. Are these interpretations correct? Here are some thoughts off the top of my head for this discussion:

1. When Paul wrote his letters, he clearly identified himself as an apostle.

2. David approached Goliath and declared what he was going to do to the giant in no uncertain terms.

3. Jesus made many claims (although sometimes veiled to hide them from unbelievers) concerning who He was and what He had come to do.

Let's examine that last point a little more closely.

A Public Figure

Jesus' family thought he was self-promoting and eager to be a public figure as we see from John 7:3-4:

> "Jesus' brothers said to him, 'Leave Galilee and go to Judea, so that your disciples there may see the works you do. No one who wants to become a public figure acts in secret. Since you are doing these things, show yourself to the world.'"

It's comforting to know that Jesus' family thought He was self-promoting, and to some extent He was—promoting that is, but without being self-centered and with a purpose. Is that possible for you and I to do the same? If Jesus was misunderstood as He carried out the Father's will for His life, then chances are we will be misunderstood as well.

Weren't Jesus' miracles a means by which He could gather a crowd to announce the coming of His kingdom? Did not the Father make Jesus a household name and a celebrity in all Israel? Did Jesus gather disciples whom He then sent out to extend His work and announce God's plan with even greater intensity and scope than He did? When Peter and John encountered the crippled man in Acts 3, they ordered him to focus his attention on them: "Peter looked straight at him, as did John. Then Peter said, 'Look at us!' So the man gave them his attention, expecting to get something from them'" (Acts 3:5-6). The apostles didn't insist, "Don't look at us, look at Jesus." They drew the man's attention to them and only then did they give him what God had in store for him through them.

We are not going to settle this issue in this chapter, but I wanted to start the dialogue with these thoughts. What do you think? Is it wrong to promote yourself? When, if ever, is it permissible? Does Philippians 2:3 prohibit any kind of ambition or marketing? I leave you to ponder these questions until the next chapter.

SELF-PROMOTION 2

We are looking at the propriety and spirituality of being more proactive as we engage in ministry and purpose opportunities. Rather than waiting on the Lord, this life philosophy assumes that God is waiting for us to decide where and how we want to be involved in serving Him and others. In the last chapter, we started a sub-series within the "Put Me In, Coach" theme. The basic issue before us is this: What is self-promotion and is it inappropriate to engage in it?

Your Light

My thought for this chapter is found in Matthew 5:14-16, where it says to do your deeds so others can see:

> "You are the light of the world. A town built on a hill cannot be hidden. Neither do people light a lamp and put it under a bowl. Instead they put it on its stand, and it gives light to everyone in the house. In the same way, let your light shine before others, that they may see your good deeds and glorify your Father in heaven."

Later in the same sermon, Jesus gave this warning:

> "Be careful not to practice your righteousness

in front of others to be seen by them. If you
do, you will have no reward from your Father
in heaven. So when you give to the needy, do
not announce it with trumpets, . . ." (Matthew
6:1-2).

Here we have an important distinction. We are not to
parade our righteous acts such as giving alms, which will
glorify self, but we are to show forth our good deeds that
will glorify God. Since God has given us our gifts and purpose that will enable us to do your good deeds, I conclude
that, in most cases, it is permissible to let people know
what we are doing and what we can do when God enables
and empowers us to do it.

Service

What's more, if God has given you gifts and a purpose and those are to be used to help others, then isn't letting people know what you can to serve them consistent
with letting your light shine, as we read above? First Peter
4:10 states, "Each of you should use whatever gift you
have received to serve others, as faithful stewards of God's
grace in its various forms." I can organize and do it quite
well since God helps me do it. Am I ever permitted to say,
"I have an organizational gift that is well developed; how
can I help you?" It seems adding the thought that my good
deeds are to serve others as well as to glorify God makes
self-promotion more acceptable and palatable than when
it is simply to show off what I can do.

I hope you will prayerfully consider what I have
written so you can develop your own personal philosophy
that will enable you to comfortably promote what God
has put into and done in your life so others can benefit
and grow. We have all been taught not to self-promote
lest pride and arrogance take root. We must be mindful
of that warning but also consider that what some refer to
as self-promotion may not be that at all. It may be giving
glory to God as we recognize what He has done and is
doing in each one of our lives.

SELF-PROMOTION 3

God has assigned you a purpose, made you creative, and given you gifts so you can do His work in creation according to your faith and size of your gift. I recently took a trip to Kenya and I took 20 people with me. I am well-known in Kenya and people readily associate me with the purpose message. Kenya represents a place where God assigned me in response to my cry, "Put me in, Coach!"

I have been on numerous local radio and television shows in Kenya, and have spoken in many churches. God opened a door for effective ministry work for me there, and I have not shrunk back or hesitated to say that God sent me there. He put me in the game and I want to play to the full stature of my abilities and gifts. As I put myself forward in Kenya, I am actually magnifying the Lord, which is the concept I want to discuss in this chapter.

Magnify the Lord

In the Old Testament, we are told to magnify the Lord. We have interpreted that simply as a matter of praise and worship when we exalt and describe God's attributes in clear and exuberant terms. Yet think about that word "magnify." Doesn't it also mean to take a small thing and make it larger, so it is easier to see and examine?

Could it mean that we are to take the smallest thing God has done through and in us and make it bigger for all to see—not with the intent to see us, but rather seeing us so people can see Him?

Is self-promotion, done with right intent, really any different than giving a testimony? When God does something for you—provides, heals, delivers, or reveals—is it wrong to stand up and say what He has done? If God has given you a gift or purpose, is it any different to broadcast the truth of what God has done or can do in and through you? And when you do, is that not the same as magnifying the Lord—taking His work in you and 'blowing it up' for all the world to see?

Intent

Self-promotion can stem from two sources: the desire to promote ourselves or the desire to further God's work through us as we serve others. Consider what Paul said in Romans 11:13-14 (NKJV): "For I speak to you Gentiles; inasmuch as I am an apostle to the Gentiles, I magnify my ministry, if by any means I may provoke to jealousy those who are my flesh and save some of them."

Paul magnified his office (other translations say "proud of, make as much as I can of, or glorify my ministry") so he could win more people to the gospel. Paul promoted what he did because God appointed him, and that made his work vital. He was not concerned with what others thought, only what God thought. He was telling the truth about himself with the right motives, and therefore he magnified himself so he could ultimately magnify the Lord.

Your job is not just to magnify the Lord by behaving yourself and not robbing banks or watching bad movies. Even heathen can do (or not do) those things. What they cannot do (but you can) is to manifest God's love for His creation through you, specifically through your purpose, gifts, and goals. Perhaps it is time you realized that your distaste for what you call self-promotion is really a means to protect yourself from criticism or being misunderstood.

It may also be an attempt to protect your privacy, for once God puts you on "front street," you lose control of your life. If God wants to put your face on a billboard, it's none of your business. Jesus and Paul 'promoted' and people criticized them; can you expect any different treatment? We will require one more chapter to look at this topic and then move on to another aspect of the *Put Me In, Coach* topic.

CHAPTER 9

SELF-PROMOTION 4

In this chapter, let's finish up our discussion of self-promotion, attempting to define what it is and if and when it is appropriate.

Two Thoughts

The two thoughts are really passages I want us to look at. The first is something Jesus said:

> "You are the light of the world. A town built on a hill cannot be hidden. Neither do people light a lamp and put it under a bowl. Instead they put it on its stand, and it gives light to everyone in the house. In the same way, let your light shine before others, that they may see your good deeds and glorify your Father in heaven" (Matthew 5:14-16).

Jesus seemed to have no problem with people letting their light shine for the glory of God. That is the challenge, for you may be asking "How do I know if I am glorifying God? What if I am glorifying self?" For that answer, let's go to something Paul wrote as he reflected on people who were self-promoting in the work of the gospel:

> It is true that some preach Christ out of envy and

rivalry, but others out of goodwill. The latter do so out of love, knowing that I am put here for the defense of the gospel. The former preach Christ out of selfish ambition, not sincerely, supposing that they can stir up trouble for me while I am in chains. *But what does it matter? The important thing is that in every way, whether from false motives or true, Christ is preached.* And because of this I rejoice (Philippians 1:15-18a, emphasis added).

There you have it: Paul did not care about the motives, only that the work of preaching the gospel was being done. Paul was looking at the bottom line or the results, and he was not going to correct someone's motives, thus hindering the good work they were doing from the wrong incentive. Others were being helped and it seems that God was using the less-than-perfect motives of the worker to get Kingdom results in people's lives. If that was good enough for Paul, it should be good enough for you and me.

People Need to Know

You should self-promote not for your benefit but for the benefit of those who are seeking who you are, what you have, and what God has empowered you to do. If you can pray and people are healed, then healed people need to know the Lord gave you the gift of healing. If you can write, then let others know you can, for someone reading your book or article may be helped and transformed through your story or ideas.

If you have died in Christ and belong to Him, then your gift, purpose, and role in society are not your choice. If God wants to make you a household name, it's none of your business. There are some members of the body who are created to be behind the scenes, but there are some who are made to be public figures. If you are private or public, it doesn't make any difference; your life is not your own. It belongs to God and therefore to others.

Let's get over any false humility that says, "If God or anyone needs me, they can come find me. I am not going to help them by self-promoting, for that is not spiritual or proper." I say, "Get over it" and let's help all those who need to see who we are and what we do to find us more easily and do so without the guilt or feeling of "self-promotion" that can go with that process. It's time to stand up and say, "This is who I am!" Will you join me or continue to hide your light under a bushel, only then to complain that no one takes you seriously? When you do, I promise you will find a new sense of joy and meaning as you trade in your season tickets for a place on the field of play.

VOLUNTEERING

As we continue to examine the "Put Me In, Coach!" theme, let's look at an interesting passage and translation: "The Lord will stretch forth Your strong scepter from Zion, saying "Rule in the midst of Your enemies." Your people will volunteer freely in the day of Your power; In holy array, from the womb of the dawn, Your youth are to You as the dew (Psalm 110:2-3 NASB). What does it meant to "volunteer freely in the day of Your power"? In fact, is it every acceptable and permissible to volunteer *without* a direction or leading of the Lord?

A Closer Look

Psalm 110 is what is known as a Messianic psalm and is often quoted in the New Testament books (23 times to be exact by seven of the nine authors), which means that Jesus would have taught the disciples from this psalm, and they in turn delivered what He said to us. Christ has fulfilled this Messianic prediction, for He is now seated at the right hand of the Father and is reigning while His enemies are being subdued under His feet. This is also the day of Christ's power, for He sent the Holy Spirit to build His church and deliver and establish His people.

Notice what His people are doing while He stretches

forth His strong scepter from Zion: They are volunteering freely. What are they volunteering to do? We are not told, but it involves warfare and battle as the entire psalm describes. When we search for a biblical example of a volunteer, my mind goes to David when he confronted the giant Goliath. Let's look there to see if we can get more insight so we can answer the question: Is it permissible to volunteer and say, "Put me in, Coach"?

God Did not Tell Him to Go

When we read 1 Samuel 17, at no time do we see that the Lord told David to attack or fight Goliath. We do read that David said he was coming to Goliath in the name of the Lord and of his vow not only to defeat Goliath, but also to cut off his head and parade it around the region. We do *not* read that the Lord or any of His representatives directed David to do what he did. This is interesting because we have other examples of David's battle strategies and they often involved asking God if he should attack and how he should do so.

This leads me to the conclusion that David volunteered to go of his own free will. He assessed the situation, weighed the probability for success, considered the rewards being offered, looked at the cowardice of the army, listened to Goliath's taunts, and after all that, said, "I'm the man. I'll go and take him on. Put me in, Coach!" We may even assume God set up this situation that was perfectly suited for David to act, but He did not tell him to act. That was up to David to decide. It seems like God wasn't upset that David acted and even helped him do what he set out to do.

I am *not* saying God does not direct our actions, for He most certainly does, but not everything has to be a word from the Lord before we act. I can't remember if the Lord directed me to write the *Monday Memo* 18 years ago. I had an idea to write and have had many theme ideas since then to produce 920 *Memos*. Has God empowered me to write for 18 years? Absolutely! Did God give me my ability to write? Of course! Did He give me specific input to write some of the *Monday Memos*? I know He did! Did He direct me to write them all? I cannot say He has.

Some weeks, I volunteered freely in the day of His power, and this day includes the explosion of social media and publishing opportunities. Eighteen years ago, I said to the Lord, "Put me in, Coach" and every Sunday when I write, my Mentor and Friend has been there to support me and help.

I leave you with these questions: If you were not afraid of missing the Lord, what would you volunteer to do today? What would you freely give yourself to in the day of His power when the battle rages for people's lives? When you get the answer, I urge you to find a way to do it and trust that if God is not in it, He will stop you. If He doesn't stop you, however, keep going and maybe 18 years from now, you will look back on something you have done, not sure if God directed you, but glad you did it nonetheless.

CHAPTER 11

VOLUNTARILY

When I was seeking the Lord to find more material for this book, I specifically asked for more biblical examples of someone volunteering to do the work of the Lord. I knew this was important because of the prevailing mindset that we are to sit and wait for directions from the Lord before we initiate activity, which assumes we can perfectly hear from the Lord and then are obediently poised to immediately carry out what we hear. Both assumptions are flawed. I am not saying the Lord never initiates or directs good deeds or direction in our lives—He most certainly does. I am saying that we have a role to play in doing things that are consistent with our purpose and creativity when God is *not* directing us.

As I was seeking, it occurred to me that I should focus on the greatest volunteer of all time, the man who volunteered to pay the highest price to do the Father's will, and that person is none other than Jesus Himself. Let's look at this concept of "Put Me In, Coach" from the Master's perspective and study His example.

Willingly

Jesus told His disciples He was the good shepherd in John 10 and made these comments in that context:

"The reason my Father loves me is that I lay down my life—only to take it up again. No one takes it from me, but I lay it down of my own accord. I have authority to lay it down and authority to take it up again. This command I received from my Father" (John 10:17-18).

Another translation says it this way:

"The Father loves me because I sacrifice my life so I may take it back again. No one can take my life from me. I sacrifice it voluntarily. For I have the authority to lay it down when I want to and also to take it up again. For this is what my Father has commanded" (John 10:17-18 NLT).

We learn in these verses that Jesus volunteered to do what He did. He did it willingly and of His own accord. The command was to expand God's flock to include Jews and Gentiles, and when Jesus heard the Father's wish, He immediately said, "Put me in, Coach! I'll do it." There was no coercion or sense of "this is what I have to do." Jesus offered Himself as a willing sacrifice, the extent to which He did is further explained by Paul.

Emptied Himself

In Paul's letter to the Philippians, he wrote about Jesus' attitude in life and ministry:

In your relationships with one another, have the same mindset as Christ Jesus: Who, being in very nature God, did not consider equality with God something to be used to his own advantage; rather, he made himself nothing by taking the very nature of a servant, being made in human likeness. And being found in appearance as a man, he humbled himself by becoming obedient to death—even death on a cross! (Philippians 2:5-8).

A seldom-referenced translation translates verse six this way: "who, existing in the form of God, did not consider equality with God as something to be used for

His own advantage" (HCSB). Jesus emptied Himself and refused to use His position and power as a means to build His own kingdom. Instead, He volunteered to carry out the assignment of the cross and we serve Him today because He did. No one coerced Him to do what He did; He did it voluntarily.

Jesus is our model for life, purpose, and ministry. In the next chapter, we will look at the implications and God's expectations for us because of what Jesus did. For now, simply consider the fact that Jesus said, "Put me in, Coach" and see where you can follow in His footsteps and do the same.

CHAPTER 12

LOVE AND JOY

In chapter eleven, we looked at the greatest volunteer of all time in our ongoing theme titled *Put Me In, Coach*! That volunteer was none other than Jesus who willingly laid down His life in response to the Father's command. We can read Paul's description of this act in Philippians 2, where Jesus emptied Himself and took on the role of a servant. Our goal as disciples is to follow Jesus and become more like Him through the process. How can we be more like Jesus and voluntarily lay down our lives? Let's work on answering that question in this chapter.

No Longer Servants

In John 15, Jesus talked to His disciples about His expectations for their lives:

> "This is to my Father's glory, that you bear much fruit, showing yourselves to be my disciples. As the Father has loved me, so have I loved you. Now remain in my love. If you keep my commands, you will remain in my love, just as I have kept my Father's commands and remain in his love. I have told you this so that my joy

may be in you and that your joy may be complete. My command is this: Love each other as I have loved you. Greater love has no one than this: to lay down one's life for one's friends. You are my friends if you do what I command. I no longer call you servants, because a servant does not know his master's business. Instead, I have called you friends, for everything that I learned from my Father I have made known to you. You did not choose me, but I chose you and appointed you so that you might go and bear fruit—fruit that will last—and so that whatever you ask in my name the Father will give you. This is my command: Love each other" (John 15:8-17).

Let's look at these words more closely.

1. Jesus expects us to bear fruit. By doing so, we will show ourselves to be His followers. Doctrine will not set us apart; fruit will.

2. Jesus does not define what the fruit is or looks like, but tells us how the fruit will be developed. We will produce a lot of fruit by keeping His commands and remaining in His love.

3. As we obey His commands, we will have His joy, which will guide our activities.

4. Jesus' commands will not direct our every action, but His commands can be summarized in one main directive: Love each other as He has loved us.

5. Once we know Jesus' commands, we understand the Father's motive for sending Jesus and that becomes the same motive He has in sending us. That motivation was and is love for people.

6. When we love others and follow our joy,

we are no longer servants being told every step we need to make and action we need to take. We are God's friends and friends do things for others not because they *have to* but because they *choose to* do so.

7. With love and joy as our motivators, we will bear fruit—willingly and of our own volition. We will pray and act, and God will give us whatever we need to bear joyful and loving fruit.

Examples

I write every day because I derive joy from doing it, and I publish what I write on social media because it may help someone. My motivation is love and joy. I travel because I love to travel; it gives me joy, and I have borne fruit all over the world as I coach, consult, and speak. My joy guides me, but my love drives me to touch as many people as possible with who I am and what God has made me to be and do. I never pray about where I go; I have told the Father to *Put Me In, Coach*, so I am never concerned that I am being misled when I am invited to go or when I decide I want to go, even if I do not feel God prompting me to do so. Don't misunderstand; He does at times prompt me, but at other times, I volunteer to go, and He meets me when I get there.

Jesus expects us to bear fruit, but He is not going to direct our every action. Our love and joy will direct some of it, and that will lead to fruit because we are fully engaged in the process. We are not held hostage by God's will; we have voluntarily offered ourselves to do it, and the results will show because we use all our energy and creativity to produce fruit. We are no longer afraid of missing God's will, for we are partners with Him (friends even) as we express who He made us to be.

In the next chapter, we will look again at Paul and how this concept played out in his life, but for now, I urge you to find your joy and express your love freely and without constraint, and do so as often as possible. As you do,

you will bear fruit and that is the end result Jesus is after in all our lives.

REWARD

Let's take another look at the concept we have been discussing, which is summarized by the phrase "Put Me in, Coach." We have been looking at our role in bearing fruit and being productive for the Lord, asking if we can actually volunteer to act or do we need to be directed by the Lord at all times. In the last two chapters, we studied Jesus' life, the greatest volunteer of all time. Now, let's look at the man who had the greatest impact on the early church after Jesus, and that is the Apostle Paul.

Voluntarily

Paul wrote to the Corinthians about his commission to preach the gospel:

> If I preach voluntarily, I have a reward; if not voluntarily, I am simply discharging the trust committed to me. What then is my reward? Just this: that in preaching the gospel I may offer it free of charge, and so not make full use of my rights as a preacher of the gospel (1 Corinthians 9:17-18).

It seems Paul was indicating it is acceptable to carry out God's will without volunteering, but it seems there is no reward for being compelled to do so. It is simply a matter of duty. Yet if we do it voluntarily, there is a reward, but not as we would think. Paul's reward was that he could volunteer to preach free of charge to those who heard.

It was customary in Paul's time for teachers and speakers to travel and receive pay for their services. Paul established that this was an acceptable practice for God's servants as well. Despite that, Paul decided to work and cover all the expenses for his team. He chose to do this, indicating it was his reward for volunteering to preach the gospel. Therefore, Paul preached voluntarily and then also volunteered to do it for free, adding the task of working for a living to his responsibilities. Paul saw his ability to work for free as his reward for volunteering to preach. That's an interesting spin on what he did, don't you think?

Freewill Offerings

In the Old Testament, there was something called a freewill offering: "These offerings are in addition to those for the Lord's Sabbaths and in addition to your gifts and whatever you have vowed and all the freewill offerings you give to the Lord" (Leviticus 23:38). This was an offering that was not prescribed or demanded but was given because the one giving it chose to do so. God did not "lay the offering" on their heart and they obeyed; they chose what they wanted to give.

I include the concept of the freewill offering because that seems to be what Paul was doing when he voluntarily preached for free. He chose of his own free will to do it. Yes, the Lord appeared on the Damascus road and said He was sending Paul to the Gentiles. When He did, Paul said in his heart, "I'll go," and then added on the part about doing it for free.

God has assigned your purpose and gifts and bestowed on you a measure of creativity. You should willingly and enthusiastically accept them and not sit back and only express them at God's direction. You should voluntarily make all those things available and accessible to other people. I am not suggesting God will not direct what He has given you; He most certainly will. At the same time, He will not direct every expression, but will wait for you to volunteer. When you do, make it an extravagant expression, just like Paul did, and receive the same reward, which is the knowledge that you are in partnership with God and the two of you make an unbeatable team.

CHAPTER 14

THE AUTHORITY OF PURPOSE

I was getting ready to teach a class not too long ago, and one of the students brought in a cake and snacks because it was her birthday. When I said, "You invited yourself to the party," it reminded me on a *Monday Memo* I wrote years ago titled, "Invite Yourself to the Party." I knew right away it fit in with our current theme, which is *Put Me In, Coach*. Let me explain with examples from my own life.

For years, I would be a guest on media shows, after which the host would rave about how well the show went, promising to have me back on the show soon. In almost every instance, I was never invited back. Now, either they were lying that the show went well (I concurred with their assessment that it did go well), or they had no intention of asking me back (which meant they were lying), or they just did not follow through (sincere but inefficient). Whatever the reason, I decided after so many disappointments to invite myself to the party: I sponsored my own weekly show on two AM stations for six years, and I also hosted hundreds of blog radio shows. What's more, I started a Vimeo channel and have many video shows posted there and on Facebook. My point is that I was no longer content to be invited to the party. Just like my student, I threw my own party.

I ran across this commentary I wrote eight years ago on Matthew 10:1-4. First, here is that passage, and then my comments:

> Jesus called his twelve disciples to him and gave them authority to drive out impure spirits and to heal every disease and sickness. These are the names of the twelve apostles: first, Simon (who is called Peter) and his brother Andrew; James son of Zebedee, and his brother John; Philip and Bartholomew; Thomas and Matthew the tax collector; James son of Alphaeus, and Thaddaeus; Simon the Zealot and Judas Iscariot, who betrayed him.

When God calls you to a purpose, He calls you by name and He calls you to Himself. It isn't just a task; it's a unique relationship with Him. I have found that when I function in my purpose, God provides for me and takes care of all I need to fulfill my purpose. He speaks to me, and my relationship with Him is somehow closer and more intimate when I am going about my purpose.

In Matthew, Jesus called twelve men to Himself and gave them authority. That was a question the Jews always asked Jesus; "By whose authority do You do these things?" Jesus did the things He did in the authority of His purpose. That is all the authority you need as well, for your purpose is your assignment from heavenly headquarters. When you move in your purpose, you don't need an invitation to the party, so to speak. You invite yourself. Someone else described it that you nominate yourself for the job.

If your purpose is to help the poor, you don't need anyone to invite you to do so. You show up where the poor are and help them. I was reflecting on this issue of authority the other day and came up with nine aspects of purpose that give you the authority to do whatever it is God wants you to do—without an invitation. Here they are:

1. **The authority of results**: Your purpose helps you bear fruit. No one can question your authority when you can show them the fruit of your labors.

2. **The authority of clarity**: Your purpose is a clear, concise statement of what you are on earth to do. People will follow and respond to you because you are direct, clear, and focused.

3. **The authority of knowledge**: Your purpose enables and even drives you to be skilled at what you do. You will have more insight and knowledge about your sphere of purpose than others.

4. **The authority of calling**: God assigned your purpose and wants you to fulfill it even more than you do. He will open doors and create opportunities for you to succeed.

5. **The authority of integrity**: Your purpose causes you to live by your values, those things that are most important to you. You don't want to undermine your purpose, so you have added incentive to be an honest person of your word.

6. **The authority of courage**: Your purpose makes you a leader where you function. You face your fears because your purpose is more important than you are. There are people waiting to benefit from what you do and who you are, so you press through obstacles to be there for them.

7. **The authority of success**: Your purpose gives you endurance to press through the barriers

and endure long periods of suffering and frequent setbacks. You don't only achieve short-term results; you do so over a long period of time, which is defined as success

8. **The authority of humility**: You know your source of strength, which is God Himself. You acknowledge your source, but you don't deny that you are good at what you do because you know God helps you produce results.

9. **The authority of honesty**: You do not engage in "false humility" (denying what you can do). You know and face your limitations and weaknesses with openness and transparency, and you do the same with your strengths.

When you have a purpose, you have all the authority you need to act. If you can't find a partner to help, you go it alone and wait for a partner to find you. If that doesn't happen, you are then content with the fact that you have the most important partner of all, the Lord Himself, and together you will attend a purpose party that will impact the lives of others and enrich your own.

CHAPTER 15

THE AUTHORITY
OF LOVE

Let's continue our quest for an answer to the question, "Is it permissible to take an active role in being creative and fulfilling purpose, or must we wait for the Lord to direct all our actions?" I am of the opinion that not only is it permissible, but also expected that we express ourselves in as many ways as possible, and I have published this book with the title, "Put Me In, Coach."

Jesus was asked, "By what authority are you doing these things? And who gave you authority to do this?" (Mark 11:28). If you step out and do more than you are currently doing, someone will ask you the same question. Let's try to find a biblical answer to the question "by whose authority?".

Shouldn't We?

Jesus instructed His disciples to love one another. How should we define or recognize this love? John defined it this way:

> If anyone has material possessions and sees a brother or sister in need but has no pity on them, how can the love of God be in that person? Dear children, let us not love with words or speech

but with actions and in truth (1 John 3:17-18).

Let's expand what John wrote to include any need a brother or sister may have. If we have experience that could benefit them, shouldn't we share it? If we have a gift that could edify them, shouldn't we express it? If we have a creative expression that could bless them, should we not produce it? Would God have to direct us to do these things, or would love dictate that we do it unless God specifically directs us *not* to do so?

Love's Authority

When asked by what authority we choose to put ourselves in the game, I maintain it is by love's authority. I am a gifted teacher, so love is all the authority I need to volunteer to teach a class. Love will motivate me to go to school or read to become a better teacher. It will drive me to watch other teachers to learn from them to be even more effective. Paul explained what I am describing this way:

> You, my brothers and sisters, were called to be free. But do not use your freedom to indulge the flesh; rather, serve one another humbly in love. For the entire law is fulfilled in keeping this one command: "Love your neighbor as yourself" (Galatians 5:13-14).

We are freed by faith, but we are to make ourselves slaves through love: "Do everything in love" (1 Corinthians 16:14).

One final thought: We don't offer to put ourselves in the game of life more often because we are afraid, pure and simple. We are afraid of missing the Lord, of getting ahead of Lord, or of disobeying the Lord. I stopped being afraid and took seriously the truth in 1 John 4:18: "There is no fear in love. But perfect love drives out fear, because fear has to do with punishment. The one who fears is not made perfect in love." Fear is a manifestation of imperfect love—for God and others. My problem when I did not act was not a fear problem but a love problem, so I asked God to expand my heart so I could love more. Today, I write, travel, and speak in love, and I put myself in the game because the Coach, my magnificent Master, has loved me enough to use me. It doesn't get any better than that.

DOING ONLY WHAT THE LORD SAYS

I was sitting in a meeting recently as someone shared with those present her creative projects. As this person described what she did, she repeatedly said, "The Lord inspired me . . . the Lord showed me . . . the Lord gave me the idea." I want to say as we start that the Lord does do all those things, as evidenced by what David said to Solomon when he handed his son the plans for the Temple: "All this," David said, "I have in writing as a result of the Lord's hand on me, and he enabled me to understand all the details of the plan" (1 Chronicles 28:19).

I do not believe, however, that the Lord does this for every creative expression. The Temple was a specific project that would impact the world until Jesus' day. In most cases, we are not talking about something that significant, but rather your purposeful creativity that involves poetry, starting a business, writing a book, or painting a picture. The Lord will bring the work to you, but it is up to your creativity to make it happen. You will function in the creativity He gave you, but you will say as Luke wrote, "With this in mind, since I myself have carefully investigated everything from the beginning, *I too decided to write an orderly account for you . . .*"(Luke 1:3a, emphasis added).

Luke decided to write and God was with him, inspiring him, but He did not dictate to him what he wrote. He was free to be Luke, using his experience, vocabulary, and ability to organize material into a cohesive account of Jesus' ministry. Luke did not claim that God told, directed, moved, or inspired him to write. He simply decided to write.

Luke said, "Put me in, Coach. I am going to do like many others and that is write an orderly account." While it sounds spiritual to attribute all your creativity and purpose expressions to the Lord, here are some reasons why that may not be wise or the way God wants you to function.

God Told Me To . . .

When we say, "God told me to do this or that," He may very well have done so, but we must be cautious not to make that an excuse for being unproductive.

1. We have all been grooved with fear by repeated warnings to "not get ahead of the Lord" or to discover "God's perfect timing." Fear does not activate but debilitates and triggers a fight-or-flight response in our brain. If we are afraid and have an idea, we will either fight it or flee from it, often employing spiritual-sounding excuses when we do either.

2. One of our fears is what other people think if we step out and do something. They may be threatened by our actions or grooved with the same fear, so we try to preempt their criticism by saying, "God told me to . . ."

3. We do not hear the Lord perfectly. Our fears and preconceived notions of who we are and what God would or would not direct us to do distort what we hear. Don't believe me? Jesus told the apostles to go and they stayed. The Father spoke from heaven endorsing Jesus' ministry and some thought it

was thunder. The Lord told Peter in Acts 10 to "kill and eat" and Peter said, "No way!" That would have required him no longer eating a kosher diet, which he assumed God would never command, and therefore, God had to tell him multiple times to kill and eat.

4. It was never God's intention that we "wait on the Lord" for every action in life, especially where our creativity and purpose are concerned. Second Corinthians 6:1 says that we are God's "coworkers." In Genesis 2:19-20, God brought all the animals before Adam so he could name them. God did not whisper in Adam's ear what to name them, but rather left it to Adam's creativity to do that. God directed Adam's work, but Adam involved who God had made him to be to complete the task.

5. We have been taught that we have a wicked heart, so we must be wary or downright hostile toward the desires in our hearts. We ignore the fact that God promised—and has followed through on that promise—to give us a new heart by His Spirit (see Ezekiel 36:26). I am not claiming our new heart is infallible, but it is not as wicked or wayward as the old one. We can trust it far more often than we currently do.

An Excuse

God has given me a gift to write and a heart to serve in Africa. I have walked with Him for 46 years, studied His Word, and learned His ways. A decade ago, I said, "Put me in, Coach" and He has done so. He has presented opportunities to me and has asked, "What are *you* going to do with these? What do *you* want to do with these?" My answer has been, "I will do as much as humanly possible by the power and energy You supply!"

God could give David the plans for the Temple and the mind to understand them because decades earlier David had composed music and poems. Then he creatively fought in the Lord's army and learned how to recognize and hear the Lord through circumstances as well as His still, small voice. Then he organized his kingdom, and finally, he was ready for even bigger things—a building the likes of which the world had never seen. As you insert yourself into "game" situations, the heavenly Coach will be able to entrust bigger and more significant opportunities to you. If you use Him as an excuse for inactivity, you will languish on the bench of life, soaking up God's love but never knowing the joys of being on the field of action.

Are you using God as an excuse not to create? Are you waiting on the Lord to do what only you can do? Do you have your marching orders, as the apostles did, but like them, are you not marching, or only marching in place? How long have you known Him, and what are you doing to prove the validity and vitality of your relationship with Him? I urge you to take a more aggressive and active role in being and expressing who God made you to be, trusting that God will direct you as you go and realizing He won't push you as you resist or continually wait on Him.

LEARNING TO TRUST YOUR HEART

As we continue our "Put Me In, Coach" theme, I want to look at the issue of our heart in this chapter, not the one that beats and keeps our blood circulating, but our inner one where our emotions, desires, and unseen parts exist. If you are looking for an exact description of what our heart is or does, you will be disappointed, for I will not attempt to explain the heart in detail, but will show why we can trust what's in our heart far more often than we have up to this point in life. At the end, you can tell me how well I did in trying to accomplish my objective.

The Heart Is Wicked: Or Is It?

I regularly hear comments or read things that warn me and the other listeners and readers to be careful when it comes to our heart. We are warned that the heart is wicked and evil and not to be trusted. The basis for this warning is found in Jeremiah 17:9 where the Lord said to the prophet, "The heart is deceitful above all things and beyond cure. Who can understand it?" We have been repeatedly warned that to trust one's heart is an invitation to sin and disaster.

Who can argue with that? We have enough life experience to know that doing what's in our heart has brought and can bring long-term negative consequences. We heed the warning and thus don't trust what's in us, requesting and demanding confirmation after confirmation before we will even begin to trust or listen to what our heart may be telling us.

The problem with all this is that we heed the warning in Jeremiah 17:9 without moving on to the next verse, where the Lord answered His own question: ""I the Lord search the heart and examine the mind, to reward each person according to their conduct, according to what their deeds deserve" (Jeremiah 17:10). it would seem from the context that God evaluates our heart matters and they are not all evil, otherwise there would be nothing to reward. God would have said, "I am here to punish all your deeds if they emanate from your heart, which is evil and beyond hope." That is not what He said.

If there may be some remnant of hope for our heart, how can we learn to trust it, for we will need our heart if we are going to live out the put-me-in-coach philosophy? The key is to acknowledge the truth in Jeremiah 17:9 but then to read what else the Lord said that pertains to our heart.

A New Heart

The Lord promised He would do a new thing in our hearts when He introduced a new covenant:

> "The days are coming," declares the Lord, "when I will make a new covenant with the people of Israel and with the people of Judah. It will not be like the covenant I made with their ancestors when I took them by the hand to lead them out of Egypt, because they broke my covenant, though I was a husband to them," declares the Lord. "This is the covenant I will make with the people of Israel after that time," declares the Lord. "I will put my law in their minds and write it on their hearts. I will be their God, and they will be my people" (Jeremiah 31:31-33).

It seems that God promised to override the operating system of our old heart with a new script (new code if you think in computer terminology). Therefore, some things in our hearts may be good, deposited there in God's own handwriting. We may have, however, an old wineskin of a heart, and Jesus said new wine cannot go into an old wineskin or the skin will burst. God took care of that problem as He explained to the prophet Ezekiel:

> "'For I will take you out of the nations; I will gather you from all the countries and bring you back into your own, and I will sprinkle clean water on you, and you will be clean; I will cleanse you from all your impurities and from all your idols. I will give you a new heart and put a new spirit in you; I will remove from you your heart of stone and give you a heart of flesh. And I will put my Spirit in you and move you to follow my decrees and be careful to keep my laws" (Ezekiel 36:24-26).

God promised a new covenant, the terms of which He would write on our hearts, and promised a new heart that would not be made of stone but of flesh. I argue that this new heart was not given to Israel in the context of a new land and temple when they returned from exile but instead was bestowed in the power of the Spirit made possible by Jesus' sacrifice on the cross.

If all this is true, then we certainly cannot trust our old heart but we can trust our new one because we can trust its creator, shepherd, and surgeon. The Lord is the one who works in our hearts and I have learned to trust the God of my heart. If it's on my heart to write, I write. If it's on my heart to go, I go. If it's on my heart to help, I help. God isn't trying to trick me and the old heart that still shows up every now and then is being gradually filled and overwritten with love messages and promptings from the Lord.

This is important if we are going to live out the "Put Me In, Coach" philosophy, for there are times when our heart moves us and we should act—should I say *must* act? May the God of your heart give you confidence not in your old heart but in the new one He has shaped and fashioned, and may you learn not to trust your heart, but the God of your heart, who will never lead you astray.

BECOMING EFFICACIOUS

It occurred to me that having the put-me-in-Coach life and work philosophy requires us to become efficacious people. Admit it, you didn't know being efficacious was to be on your bucket list. If you are really honest, you may admit you don't even know what it means. That's fine, for I didn't know until about 15 years ago, but when I discovered the definition, I determined to become more efficacious with God's help. Let's look at the word and then an application for this chapter's lesson.

Efficacy

The word efficacy simply means you have the belief that you can make something happen or cause something to take place. Whenever you have an idea, you are making an efficacy appraisal, determining whether or not you can make that idea become a reality. If you think, "I should go back to school," you begin your efficacy appraisal and either talk yourself into the reality or out of it. You either think, "Yes, that will be enjoyable. I have wanted to do that for a while," or "My God, I haven't been in school for 20 years. I don't do well in math. I don't have the time. I don't have the money. This can't be the Lord."

Do you see how it works? Either you use your

thinking and self-talk to move toward making something happen or away from making something happen. You become either efficacious or inefficacious. It is important that you learn to trust your thoughts if you are going to be efficacious. If you continually reject them as foreigners and alien beings to be feared and eradicated, you are destined for an inefficacious life and walk with the Lord.

You probably never have the thought, "I should be an astronaut or a nuclear scientist." Those two things would be out of the realm of possibility for you. Most of the ideas you have are related to something you have the capacity to do or learn to do. Your thought of going back to school would be for something you would enjoy learning: "I have wanted to study the Bible or art or psychology; this will be my chance." God isn't trying to trick or entrap you; He is working with you to make you the best and most productive person possible. With that confidence, you can say, "Put me in school, Coach! Put me in ministry, Coach! Put me in missions, Coach! Put me in business, Coach!" That attitude will make you an efficacious person.

An Example

In the book of Acts, Paul and his team were praying for the Lord to put them in the game of missions. They had been trying to go in one direction, but the Spirit of Jesus did not permit them to go:

> Paul and his companions traveled throughout the region of Phrygia and Galatia, having been kept by the Holy Spirit from preaching the word in the province of Asia. When they came to the border of Mysia, they tried to enter Bithynia, but the Spirit of Jesus would not allow them to. So they passed by Mysia and went down to Troas. During the night Paul had a vision of a man of Macedonia standing and begging him, "Come over to Macedonia and help us." After Paul had seen the vision, we got ready at once to leave for Macedonia, concluding that God had called us to preach the gospel to them (Acts 16:6-10).

What can we learn from this passage to help us be efficacious? The team was actively seeking the Lord, and were in motion trying to find the open door. They trusted the Lord was with them, wanting them to go and be in the game. When Paul had the dream, he was confident it was not a trick. The vision he had was not outlandish, but something they could and wanted to do. Then was the most important step in the story: they got ready to act. They did not need more confirmation or time to wait on the Lord. They packed their bags and became efficacious, causing the vision Paul had to become a reality.

Are you probing and experimenting to discover what position God wants you to play in the game? When you have an idea, are you immediately looking for a way to make it happen? Do you trust the Lord to guide and not trick or mislead you? If you answer yes to those questions, then you are on your way to becoming an efficacious person. If not, you have some work to do so you can stop being the biggest obstacle between you and the Lord's will for your life.

God is with you and not against you. Armed with that knowledge, you can be confident to step out and into the game, no matter what game God has assigned to you. When you do that, you will be God's partner as together you work to make a mark in the world only you two can make. When you don't do that, you will devote your energy and creativity to block instead of enhance God's purpose for you. The choice is yours and I pray you choose efficacy.

CHAPTER 19

ONE MORE TIME

The Bible is full of surprises concerning the people God used to accomplish His purposes. We have looked at some of them in this book, men like Peter, Nehemiah, and Moses. Perhaps the unlikeliest of all was a man whose name was mentioned in Hebrews 11, the faith hall-of-fame chapter: 32 And what more shall I say? For time will fail me if I tell of Gideon, Barak, Samson, Jephthah, of David and Samuel and the prophets" (Hebrews 11:32). The name I want to focus on is Samson, for he would have had trouble being a member of some churches let alone a champion of God. That is exactly what he was, however, so let's look at his story in this chapter and see when and how he manifested the Put Me In, Coach mentality.

A Strong Man

Samson is known for his strength, the secret of which was his total commitment to God's purpose for his life, as evidenced by what was referred to as a Nazirite vow:

> The angel of the Lord appeared to her and said, "You are barren and childless, but you are going to become pregnant and give birth to a son.

Now see to it that you drink no wine or other fermented drink and that you do not eat anything unclean. You will become pregnant and have a son whose head is never to be touched by a razor because the boy is to be a Nazirite, dedicated to God from the womb. He will take the lead in delivering Israel from the hands of the Philistines" (Judges 13:3-5).

We won't develop the concept of this unusual vow not to cut hair or drink wine, but suffice it to say that Samson had a purpose (deliver Israel from the hands of the Philistines and was especially gifted to accomplish it. It seems the Lord would come upon him mightily (see Judges 14:19 and 15:14), and he would perform feats of superhuman strength. One translation says that the Lord would clothe Himself with Samson, which is a great image of how God uses any of us in our purpose, It's He who is doing the work, but it looks like us as we cooperate with His will.

Like all purpose champions, however, Samson had a weakness and it was women. He ended up marrying a Philistine woman named Delilah who was not a good influence on him, and eventually she nagged Samson into telling her the secret of his strength:

So he told her everything. "No razor has ever been used on my head," he said, "because I have been a Nazirite dedicated to God from my mother's womb. If my head were shaved, my strength would leave me, and I would become as weak as any other man." When Delilah saw that he had told her everything, she sent word to the rulers of the Philistines, "Come back once more; he has told me everything." So the rulers of the Philistines returned with the silver in their hands. After putting him to sleep on her lap, she called for someone to shave off the seven braids of his hair, and so began to subdue him. And his strength left him. Then she called, "Samson, the Philistines are upon you!" He awoke from his sleep and thought, "I'll go out as before and shake myself free." But he did not know that the Lord had left him. Then the Philistines seized him, gouged out his eyes and took him down to Gaza. Binding him with bronze shackles, they set him to grinding grain in the prison. But the hair on his head began to grow again after it had been shaved (Judges 16:17-22).

By now, you may be wondering how this story relates to the Put Me In, Coach theme of this book. For the answer, we have to look at a little more of the story.

One More Time

Samson had failed, succumbing to a serious character flaw that led to his defeat and humiliation. Samson is listed in Hebrews 11 as a man of faith and it was when he was at his worst that he became his best, when he said, "Put me in, Coach!"

> Then Samson prayed to the Lord, "Sovereign Lord, remember me. Please, God, strengthen me just once more, and let me with one blow get revenge on the Philistines for my two eyes." Then Samson reached toward the two central pillars on which the temple stood. Bracing himself against them, his right hand on the one and his left hand on the other, Samson said, "Let me die with the Philistines!" Then he pushed with all his might, and down came the temple on the rulers and all the people in it. Thus he killed many more when he died than while he lived (Judges 16:28-30).

Samson had one-more-time faith that caused him to ask for another chance to do what he had been created to do. It is amazing that God heard his plea and clothed Himself one more time in Samsons purpose.

The lessons from this story are many, but for our purposes, there is only one. Even after his greatest failure, when he was at his lowest point and it seemed like it was all over, Samson had put-me-in-coach faith. He inserted himself in the game and God used him to bring about a victory for his people. If Samson said, "Put me in, Coach," then you can, too. Have you allowed your failures and disappointments to intimidate your will and desire to be used by God? Do you think it's too late for you to play a meaningful role in God's game of purpose? If you answer yes to either question, then take the lesson from this chapter and follow Samson's example. Put your right and left hands to the pillars of your purpose, push with all the might God gives you, and then feel the earth shake under the power of your purpose. It's not too late, unless you determine it is.

CHAPTER 20

FREEWILL MEANS FREE WILL

As we close out our "Put Me In, Coach" studies, we are still trying to answer the question: Is it ever appropriate to see a situation and volunteer to be involved even if we do not sense the leading of the Lord? I have tried to make a case that it is and here is one more argument to help prove my case.

An Offering

When Moses laid the plans before the people for the Wilderness tabernacle, he said it would be necessary to take an offering to the Lord to meet the construction cost. Here is how the people responded:

> Then the whole Israelite community withdrew from Moses' presence, and *everyone who was willing* and whose heart moved them came and brought an offering to the Lord for the work on the tent of meeting, for all its service, and for the sacred garments. *All who were willing,* men and women alike, came and brought gold jewelry of all kinds: brooches, earrings, rings and ornaments. They all presented their gold as a wave offering to the Lord . . . *All the Israelite*

men and women who were willing brought to
the Lord *freewill offerings* for all the work the
Lord through Moses had commanded them to
do (Exodus 35:20-23, 29, emphasis added).

The phrase "who were willing" is used three times
as Moses described how the people responded. Therefore,
what they gave was designated a freewill offering because
the Lord did not direct them how much to give. He only directed them to give and left how much up to each individ-
ual. He did not say, "Give what you want," and then as the
people contemplated the amount, the Lord did not whisper, "Ten talents of gold," only then to have the person
give ten talents in obedience. That would not have been a
freewill offering. It would have been a *willing* offering if
the giver's heart was right, but not a *freewill* gift.

A Practical Application

Therefore, we see that it was acceptable for the
people to determine how much and what they were going
to give toward the tabernacle. Can we apply this same
principle to our situation today? We are building the
church of Jesus and He has laid out what needs to be done.
We have received gifts from the Spirit and we each have
a purpose to develop and fulfill in a way that will bring us
joy and benefit and serve other people. If it was appropriate to give an offering of money or wealth for the tabernacle, why would it be inappropriate for us to give a freewill
offering of who we are and what we do to the Lord's work
as our hearts move us?

What's more, since we are to exercise dominion
over the earth as commanded in Genesis 1:28-29, why
would it be inappropriate to offer those same gifts and talents to make the world a better place to the glory of God?
Would God really be offended if you decided to help 50
orphans in Africa as an offering of thanks for His care
and provision for your family? Do you think the Lord
would respond, "Who told you to help 50 orphans? I only
wanted you to help 10 orphans and let the other 40 suffer.
How dare you step out of My will to do good? I am the

boss around here, and you will do what I tell you to do—no more and no less."

That may sound preposterous, but it seems some believe if they get ahead of the Lord or do too much good or go too far that God will be displeased. My thinking is if God gave me a gift to write, then I must work to make that gift as good as it can be and then use it as often as possible. I spent nine years writing a verse-by-verse devotional of the entire New Testament. I started my publishing company to help other people write because I am a writer. It is a freewill offering of my gift to God's people to help them express their creativity and know the joy of having a published work. Did I go too far? Did I give too much? Am I outside the boundaries of what God permits? I will let you be the judge of that, while I continue to publish and write.

My point is that freewill means just that. We are to use our own judgment to freely and willingly give what we have and who we are to the world around us, both the church and society. God is not looking for slaves, although He does direct our work and at times will be quite specific about what He wants us to do and with whom. There are other times when the Lord poses the question, "What do you want to do?" and I maintain it is permissible to respond, "Put me in, Coach!" After that, you need only look at the needs around you and put your hand to the work. God won't be threatened. To the contrary, you will honor Him by so doing, and you in turn will find the joy of doing something not because you *have* to do it but because you *choose* to do it. God wants partners and friends, not slaves, so be God's friend and express who you are. You will be glad you did.

DON'T BE A FOOL

By now, you get my point (I hope). We need to involve ourselves more aggressively in doing the work God has for us to do. Many of us have been too passive and cautious to say, "Here I am, Lord, use me." even volunteering if we don't see a door open. Let's now look at the role that others can play in helping us put ourselves in the game.

A Fool

Not too long ago, I was editing an entry from my daily Proverbs devotional that focused on this verse: "He who trusts in himself is a fool, but he walks in wisdom is kept safe" (28:26). If you are like me, you have read that verse to have a negative meaning that if we trust in ourselves, we will go astray or get into trouble because what is in us is wrong due to our tendency to be deceived. Is there another way to interpret that verse? There is and here is what I wrote about that verse.

It is easy to underestimate your potential and the power of your ideas. That's the reason you need other people speaking into your life if you are to walk in wisdom so they can help you not only see your weaknesses but also your strengths. Who are your coaches and mentors? Who challenges and broadens your perspective on life and purpose? Who is on your personal "board of directors"? As an example of the kind of input and encouragement you need from others, read about the encounter Jonathan and David had in 1 Samuel 23:16-18:

> And Saul's son Jonathan went to David at Horesh and helped him find strength in God. "Don't be afraid," he said. "My father Saul will not lay a hand on you. You will be king over Israel, and I will be second to you. Even my father Saul knows this." The two of them made a covenant before the Lord. Then Jonathan went home, but David remained at Horesh.

Jonathan did not visit David to rebuke him or tell him he was doing something wrong. He came to remind David of the promise of God and to encourage him not to give up. Jonathan affirmed the call and David's role in serving the nation, even though David lived under a death threat from Saul, which helped keep David on the right path. Yes, we may need people to correct us when we are wrong, but we often need them to encourage us to accept our own greatness and brilliance in the area of our gifts and purpose. You are a fool if you don't listen to people who tell you what you are doing right and encourage you to do more of it.

An Assessment

About 13 years ago, I volunteered to have what's called a 360-degree evaluation done on me. I chose 30 people who completed an online survey that evaluated me, my leadership, and my character in 29 different areas. It was a long and complicated assessment, which I also completed, answering the same questions. When I got the results, it scored me in areas like collaboration, community care, communication, personal growth, passivity, and cooperation, among others.

The scores came back on a complicated circle graph that had dark gray areas in each category with a red line somewhere in that category as well. The red line was where I saw myself and the gray area was where others saw me to be. Without exception, my red line fell below the gray areas of others in every positive category, but that line was above the gray areas in the negative characteristics. What did this indicate? It showed I consistently overestimated my weaknesses and underestimated my strengths.

I was stunned by the results, but I heard the Lord in them. He was telling me to stop playing small, to stop being "Christian" by being humble. My humility of considering myself less than the real me was actually false and denied what the Lord had done in my life and who He had made me to be. After I examined the results, I determined I was not going to shrink back, not be "Christian" (and by that, I mean the wrong interpretation of what it meant to be realistic concerning my gifts and talents) and act like everything depended on God as if I had no role in His plan for my life. From that point, I decided to publish and broadcast *everything* I knew and seize *every* opportunity to make myself available to help as many people as possible.

As I walked out of a church not too long ago in Nairobi, a church I had not visited in many years, I was greeted by three women (and it is a church of thousands) who told me how I had changed their lives when I met with them in 2005-2006. They gave me their stories, wanted my card, and promised to reconnect with me. I was surprised because I thought my impact was forgotten there due to my prolonged absence. It had not, and I am now more determined than ever to renew my efforts to play big and live by the "Put Me In, Coach" philosophy.

I invite you to join me because my guess is you are just like I was: underestimating your capacity for God's work and purpose and how that will impact others for good. Don't play small and hide in the crowd, insisting that if God wants you, He will have to find you (and you won't make it easy for Him to do). Present yourself to the Lord in the fullness of who you are and make a difference while you still have time. Find other people, coaches, mentors, friends, or whoever it is who can and will help you live up to your potential and not live down to your fears. Don't be a fool and only trust yourself where your strengths are concerned. Listen to what God has been trying to tell you through others and don't stubbornly cling to your negative view on who you are and what you can do. If you do that, the best for you is yet to come. If you don't do that, then get used to the view from the bench, for that is where you will sit as you watch others play the game of purpose.

HIDING

When I read, meditate, and coach and counsel reluctant people, I see the need to fortify this life philosophy in you (and to some extent in me). In the next four chapters, let's look at two bad examples of the put-me-in-coach philosophy (King Saul and Moses), and two good examples (Nehemiah and the Apostle Paul). Let's start with King Saul.

Confirmation

I often hear people say to me, "If God would show me His will, if I really knew it's what He wanted, I would be glad to do it. I will go to Africa with you, write, preach, or start a business—once I am certain it is His will." I have had many experiences with people who say this but then ignore the signs before them that they are to act. Sometimes they are polite but at other times they adamantly refuse to budge, wanting to do (or not do) what they are considering on their own terms and according to their own timetable. They have no urgency and no intention of moving out of their comfort zone.

These folks cause me to think of King Saul. There is no one who had more miraculous confirmations concerning God's will for his life than Saul. These verses explain why I make that statement:

> Then Samuel took a flask of olive oil and poured it on Saul's head and kissed him, saying, "Has not the Lord anointed you ruler over his inheritance? When you leave me today, you will meet two men near Rachel's tomb, at Zelzah on the border of Benjamin. They will say to you, 'The donkeys you set out to look for have been found. And now your father has stopped thinking about them and is worried about you. He is asking, "What shall I do about my son?"'

> "Then you will go on from there until you reach the great tree of Tabor. Three men going up to worship God at Bethel will meet you there. One will be carrying three young goats, another three loaves of bread, and another a skin of wine. They will greet you and offer you two loaves of bread, which you will accept from them.

> "After that you will go to Gibeah of God, where there is a Philistine outpost. As you approach the town, you will meet a procession of prophets coming down from the high place with lyres, timbrels, pipes and harps being played before them, and they will be prophesying. The Spirit of the Lord will come powerfully upon you, and you will prophesy with them; and you will be changed into a different person. Once these signs are fulfilled, do whatever your hand finds to do, for God is with you" (1 Samuel 10:1-7).

Would you say that God confirmed His desires for Saul's life? And once He did, notice the wonderful put-me-in-coach mandate the Lord gave him: "Do whatever your hand finds to do." God anointed and commissioned Saul and then told him to go do whatever he found that needed to be done. What was Saul's response? Did he run forth to free his people? Did he feed the poor? Set the captives free? No, he did none of those things; in fact, he ran the other way.

When Saul returned home from his lost-donkey search, his uncle asked him where he had been and what Samuel had said to him. Saul answered, "'He assured us that the donkeys had been found.' But he did not tell his uncle what Samuel had said about the kingship" (1 Samuel 10:16). I find it odd Saul would not report the exciting news that he had been selected to be the next king. Was he reluctant to draw attention to himself? Was he being modest and humble? Did he not want to offend his father, who perhaps wanted to be king one day? We don't know for sure, but we find a clue later in the chapter:

> When Samuel had all Israel come forward by tribes, the tribe of Benjamin was taken by lot. Then he brought forward the tribe of Benjamin, clan by clan, and Matri's clan was taken. Finally Saul son of Kish was taken. But when they looked for him, he was not to be found. So they inquired further of the Lord, "Has the man come here yet?" And the Lord said, "Yes, he has hidden himself among the supplies" (1 Samuel 10:20-22).

After everything that had transpired to confirm Saul's role, we learn that he was hiding among the baggage. He was concealing himself in the everyday clutter of life because he was either afraid to become king or he simply did not want the position. Seeing what he had seen was not enough to motivate Saul; being among the prophets and prophesying was not enough; hearing from the great man of God was not enough. He still hid despite all the confirmations and super-spiritual events. (Also, note that the Lord knew exactly where Saul was and was only too happy to reveal his location to others. You may think you are hiding from the Lord, but you are not.)

How about you? Are you hiding? Are you making

it difficult for God and others to find and involve you in work you are capable of doing? Are you still sitting on the sidelines after frequent thoughts of what you would want to do for the Lord? Have you thought of doing what your hand finds to do, only to shrink back in fear or indecision? Ask the Lord if you are guilty of following in Saul's footsteps by playing hide and seek with the Lord. If He indicates you are, then stop waiting for an engraved invitation and instead put yourself in the game, not worrying about missing the Lord by doing too much, but concerned that you will miss Him by doing too little.

DON'T PUT ME IN, COACH

In the last chapter, we looked at King Saul and his reluctance to step up and out to fulfill God's purpose for his life. Now let's look at Moses, but you may be surprised to learn that he was also reluctant to put himself in the game, so much so that the Lord's anger burned against him. Let's see how all that played out in Moses' story and life.

Excuses

When God spoke to him from the bush, Moses' first comment was, "Here I am!" He seemed ready to do what God wanted before He knew what it was, an attitude we would do well to imitate. But wait. Moses offered his first excuse when he asked, "Who am I?' I relate that question to our tendency to discount our ability to accomplish our purpose when we find out what it is.

Later, Moses' second excuse was, "Suppose I go to the Israelites and say to them, 'The God of your fathers has sent me to you,' and they ask me, 'What is his name?' Then what shall I tell them?" (Exodus 3:13). Moses was coming up with the excuse that he wasn't ready and didn't know enough about God, so he could not go. His third excuse was: "What if they do not believe me or listen to me and say, 'The Lord did not appear to you'?" (Exodus

4:1). This question indicated that Moses was concerned he would fail, which is a common hindrance to being purposeful and creative for all of us.

Moses' fourth excuse is implied by the Lord's next comment: "Then the Lord said to him, 'What is that in your hand?' 'A staff,' he [Moses] replied" (Exodus 4:2). God was teaching Moses to use what he had and not to fret over what he didn't have, which is another common excuse (I don't have enough education, or money, or knowledge, or resources). Moses' fifth excuse was: "Moses said to the Lord, 'O Lord, I have never been eloquent, neither in the past nor since you have spoken to your servant. I am slow of speech and tongue'" (Exodus 4:10). With this excuse, Moses had moved from honest questioning to procrastination. He was working hard to come up with some excuse, *any* excuse, so he wouldn't have to go to Egypt.

When we look at Moses' final comment at the burning bush, we see that Moses, having expressed five excuses, simply refused to go to Egypt. "But Moses said, 'O Lord, please send someone else to do it'" (Exodus 4:13). In essence, Moses said no to God! Moses refused to go and basically saying, "Don't put me in, Coach."

What was God's response? "Then the Lord's anger burned against Moses" (Exodus 4:14). Up to this point in the story, God was patient and gracious with Moses, responding to all his objections. After Moses' refusal to go, however, God was angry. I hope I never make God that angry, but this story proves it can happen. God is patient but there are limitations to His patience, and we are never quite sure when we will push Him to that extreme.

Missing Purpose

People ask me all the time, "Can you refuse your purpose?" and my answer is always a resounding yes. Consider these two passages

1. But the Pharisees and experts in the law rejected God's purpose for themselves (Luke 7:30).

2. As God's fellow workers we urge you not

to receive God's grace in vain (2 Corinthians 6:1-2).

You can receive the grace of God's purpose in vain, choosing to ignore or do nothing with it. You can sit on your gifts and remain in the comfort zone of life rather than experience the discomfort of new faith experiences. You can also be so afraid of doing the wrong thing that you choose to do nothing. God had answered and addressed each of Moses' questions and concerns, so the real reason for Moses' reluctance could be revealed: Moses simply didn't want to do it.

How about you? Are you testing God's patience through delays and excuses? The good news is that after Moses gave his final answer, God assigned Aaron to go with him and sent them both on their way to Egypt where they changed the course of history. If you confess you don't want to fulfill your purpose, admitting you are scared, lazy, or lack confidence, then the Lord will still help you.

You are not alone in your PurposeQuest; God is with you, even if you are hesitant. All you have to do is acknowledge where you are and ask God's help. He will do the rest. Let this be the time in your life when you face reality and still move on to do great things for God, just like Moses did.

CHAPTER 24

MAKE YOURSELF AVAILABLE

In the previous two chapters, we looked at bad examples of what I am calling the "Put Me In, Coach" mentality. People with that mindset are not only ready to be used by God, they are also aggressively seeking ways to be used, making themselves available. Our bad examples the last two chapters were King Saul and Moses, but our two good examples are Nehemiah and the Apostle Paul (who we have already looked at, but we have more insight to garner from his life). Right now, let's look at Nehemiah.

Passion

When Nehemiah heard some visitors' answers to his questions about the conditions in Jerusalem, he was deeply moved: "When I heard these things, I sat down and wept. For some days I mourned and fasted and prayed before the God of heaven" (Nehemiah 1:4-5).

When I speak or write, I sometimes substitute the word passion for purpose. Passion is a driving force that activates your creativity and will to do something. Tears of joy and sorrow often accompany that passion as you respond and make yourself vulnerable and available to a need in the world. The first time I spoke about purpose, people in the room wept. I have seen thousands more cry

over the years. Tears and purpose seem to go hand in hand.

In 1998, I was watching a television documentary about the suffering of women in Afghanistan and began to cry. I remember praying, "Lord, why am I crying? I don't know anyone there, but if you need someone to go to Afghanistan, I'm willing." Out of the blue in 2003, I received an invitation to go to Afghanistan from people I didn't even know. I went and it changed my life and the course of my ministry.

Clarity

Nehemiah prayed and fasted to clarify his passion and way forward. Then his big break came. One day he was serving the king and the king noticed that Nehemiah was sad. Let's read the rest in Nehemiah's own words.

> The king said to me, "What is it you want?" Then I prayed to the God of heaven, and I answered the king, "If it pleases the king and if your servant has found favor in his sight, let him send me to the city in Judah where my fathers are buried so that I can rebuild it." Then the king, with the queen sitting beside him, asked me, "How long will your journey take, and when will you get back?" It pleased the king to send me; so I set a time. I also said to him, "If it pleases the king, may I have letters to the governors of Trans-Euphrates, so that they will provide me safe-conduct until I arrive in Judah? And may I have a letter to Asaph, keeper of the king's forest, so he will give me timber to make beams for the gates of the citadel by the temple and for the city wall and for the residence I will occupy?" And because the gracious hand of my God was upon me, the king granted my requests. So I went to the governors of Trans-Euphrates and gave them the king's letters. The king had also sent army officers and cavalry with me (Nehemiah 2:4-9).

When the king asked Nehemiah what he wanted, Nehemiah had a ready answer. The king understood what he wanted and could then either say yes or no. There seemed to be no hesitancy or ambivalence on Nehemiah's part because he had prayed and thought out what he wanted to do.

Also, notice how little religious jargon there was in his dialogue with the king. Yes, Nehemiah did admit he prayed and God's gracious hand was upon him, but besides that, he was remarkably natural: "Send me . . . so I can rebuild." "I set a time." "May I have letters?" God was not offended or put off by Nehemiah's desire to help the city of his fathers. At no time do we see that God told Nehemiah to go. He made himself available to go, and asked God's and the king's help.

What do you have a passion to do? What problem do you have a passion to address? Are you clear about what you want to do to engage that passion? I urge you to get the kind of clarity Nehemiah had, and then pray, "Put me in, Coach." After that, watch for the door to open and see it as God's help so you can participate in the matter close to your heart. Nehemiah had nothing but success when he went home, and you can expect that can kind of success as well, but only if you follow your heart to put yourself in the game where it is most meaningful for you.

THINKING THE THOUGHTS OF GOD

For our last chapter, let's go back and look at the Apostle Paul's life that is a good example of the put-me-in-coach mentality.

The Mind of Christ

Paul wrote this to the Corinthians church:

This is what we speak, not in words taught us by human wisdom but in words taught by the Spirit, explaining spiritual realities with Spirit-taught words. The person without the Spirit does not accept the things that come from the Spirit of God but considers them foolishness, and cannot understand them because they are discerned only through the Spirit. The person with the Spirit makes judgments about all things, but such a person is not subject to merely human judgments, for, "Who has known the mind of the Lord so as to instruct him?" *but we have the mind of Christ* (1 Corinthians 2:12-16, emphasis added).

Paul made the remarkable statement that he and his co-workers had the mind of Christ. Does that mean we have it, too? If we do, why are we so surprised, because the Spirit resides in us to lead and guide us into all truth (see John 16:13)? How long does it take to obtain this mind of Christ? Ten years? Twenty years? Longer? It seems that Paul had it almost immediately:

> Saul spent several days with the disciples in Damascus. *At once*, he began to preach in the synagogues that Jesus is the Son of God. All those who heard him were astonished and asked, "Isn't he the man who raised havoc in Jerusalem among those who call on this name? And hasn't he come here to take them as prisoners to the chief priests?" Yet Saul grew more and more powerful and baffled the Jews living in Damascus by proving that Jesus is the Messiah (Acts 9:19-22, emphasis added).

The mind of Christ is not achieved after long periods of study and discipleship. Paul almost immediately went to work to preach, proving from the Old Testament that Jesus was and is the Christ. Is there a chance that you have the mind of Christ, but are afraid to say so because you have been taught to be careful and assume what is in you is worthless? If so, then let's look at some concepts to help you accept that what you are thinking is from the Lord, and is sufficient to ask God to put you in the game.

Agreeable to His Will

The Amplified Version translates Proverbs 16:3 in these words: "Roll your works upon the Lord [commit and trust them wholly to Him; He will cause your thoughts to become agreeable to His will, and] so shall your plans be established and succeed" (AMPC). This process of having God's thoughts may seem so natural that you suspect it cannot possibly be spiritual. Thus, you to wait for a more dramatic encounter with God's voice so you will be certain of its authenticity. That is not what occurred in Luke's life when he set out to write his gospel:

> Many have undertaken to draw up an account

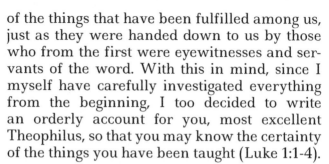

of the things that have been fulfilled among us, just as they were handed down to us by those who from the first were eyewitnesses and servants of the word. With this in mind, since I myself have carefully investigated everything from the beginning, I too decided to write an orderly account for you, most excellent Theophilus, so that you may know the certainty of the things you have been taught (Luke 1:1-4).

Luke did not say that the Lord directed him to write or report that he had a heavenly visitation commanding him to write. Luke said, "I decided to write." Luke had the mind of Christ. He put himself in the game of writing, so to speak, and the Spirit inspired his words—yet he interpreted the experience as his decision to write.

Do you have any ideas, something that has been in your mind and heart for a while, or something that is more recent? Have you delayed on the older ideas, hoping they would go away? Have you dismissed the newer ideas because they may be a trick of your own mind, or worse yet, of the devil himself? Either way, you may be missing the point that you have the mind of Christ and your ideas, old or new, may actually be agreeable to His will.

As we close this book, I hope you are more eager to be productive by making yourself available for God to use you. I trust that you have seen that fear is our common enemy, causing us to shrink back instead of move forward with confidence. I will continue to ask the Coach to put me in the game, and I trust that as I go in, I will look up and see you joining me so we can play on the same team and enjoy our victories together. Until then, I ask you to at least consider that you are thinking the thoughts of God so you can find a reason to act on them instead of sitting on the sidelines while you critique and evaluate them.

CONCLUDING
THOUGHTS

I hope I have made a compelling case that your walk with the Lord is not the equivalent of a robot or drone that receives a signal from an external source, but rather a partnership. God is looking for friends and not servants, although we are all His servants in a general sense, primed to follow His lead and do His will whenever He speaks or directs. I have made it clear that God does indeed do this, directing our thoughts and actions to achieve His works and fulfill His purpose. There are other times, however, when God puts us in situations and it's up to us to make the most of them.

I was walking the other morning and listening to a book by John M. Satterfield titled *Cognitive Behavioral Therapy: Techniques for Retraining Your Brain.* With 6:17 left in the audio book, Satterfied included this quote from John Gardner, I am assuming the man who wrote a classic book on leadership:

Meaning is not something you stumble across, like the answer to a riddle or the prize in a treasure hunt. Meaning is something you build into your life. You build it out of your own past, out of your affections and loyalties, out of your own talent and understanding, out of things you believe in, out of the things and people you love, and out of the values for which you are willing to sacrifice something.

I thought that quote spoke to what I have been writing about in this book. We are to take the purpose that God assigns us and make it into something, using our creativity, experience, and gifts in the process. We listen for God's voice, but sometimes His voice is in what we see, which we assume everyone can see but usually cannot. If I see chaos, I am going to view that differently than most, because my purpose is to create order out of the chaos. Someone else may see the situation and think, *That's a mess*, while I think, *How can I create order?* I then direct my thoughts and energy to do so, trusting that God is with me and will help me.

It all boils down to removing any fear we may have when we serve the Lord. I am not afraid God is going to trick me and lead me where I should not go. I am not afraid that He is trying to entrap me by tempting or teasing me with a tantalizing scenario, only to punish me when I step forward to do something with it. I am not afraid that I can get ahead of Him (but I do believe I can lag behind Him, sluggishly responding to opportunities He places before me). I am not afraid I am overstepping my boundaries, for He will correct me if I do (but where purpose is concerned, my boundaries are broad—and so are yours). I am not insinuating that I have conquered fear, but I recognize its role in my life, and I confront it so it will not limit what God or I can do at any given time.

I challenge you to create meaning in your life, as John Gardner advised in his quote. Take who you are, what you have done, where you have been, and what God has taught you, mix them all together, and bake a purpose cake. Then write on the cake, *Put Me In, Coach* and share a piece of purpose cake with your friends. More importantly, cut a big piece for yourself. Celebrate the fact that God has not left your house desolate but has laid before you many exciting opportunities to serve Him and others in the power of your purpose and creativity. I look forward to playing with you on the field of purpose so that together we may glorify God by winning the game and "completing the work He gave [us] to do," just like Jesus did (see John 17:4).

Keep in Touch
with John W. Stanko

www.purposequest.com
www.johnstanko.us
www.stankobiblestudy.com
www.stankomondaymemo.com
or via email at johnstanko@gmail.com

John also does extensive relief and
community development work in Kenya.
You can see some of his projects at
www.purposequest.com/contributions

PurposeQuest International
PO Box 8882
Pittsburgh, PA 15221-0882

Additional Titles by John W. Stanko

A Daily Dose of Proverbs
A Daily Taste of Proverbs
Changing the Way We Do Church
I Wrote This Book on Purpose
Life Is A Gold Mine: Can You Dig It?
Strictly Business
The Faith Files, Volume 1
The Faith Files, Volume 2
The Faith Files, Volume 3
The Leadership Walk
The Price of Leadership
Unlocking the Power of Your Creativity
Unlocking the Power of Your Productivity
Unlocking the Power of Your Purpose
Unlocking the Power of You
What Would Jesus Ask You Today?
Your Life Matters

Live the Word Commentary: Matthew
Live the Word Commentary: Mark
Live the Word Commentary: Luke
Live the Word Commentary: John
Live the Word Commentary: Acts
Live the Word Commentary: Romans
Live the Word Commentary: 1 & 2 Corinthians
Live the Word Commentary: Galatians, Ephesians,
Philippians, Colossians, Philemon
Live the Word Commentary: 1 & 2 Thessalonians,
1 & 2 Timothy, and Titus
Live the Word Commentary: Hebrews
Live the Word Commentary: Revelation

Made in the USA
Las Vegas, NV
02 February 2022

42876644R00056